T0019058

First Love

&

Other Poems

Me▬▬rical Moments for the Most of Us

Norman Weinstein

Beau Soleil Publishing

©2015 Norman Weinstein. All rights reserved.

No part of this book may be reproduced in any form
or in any means, electronic or mechanical, including
photocopying, recording, or by any information storage
and retrieval system, without permission in writing from
the publisher.

Cover art by Emily Eve Weinstein
Cover design by Emily Eve Weinstein
Book design by JoAnne Thompson

10 9 8 7 6 5 4 3 2 1

Printed in the United States of America

ISBN-13: 978-0-9864267-2-8

Beau Soleil Publishing
An imprint of Publishers Place, Inc
821 Fourth Avenue - Suite 201
Huntington West Virginia 25701

www.publishersplace.org

For my wife Deborah and our three children
Rachel, Emily and Jonathan

CONTENTS

FIRST LOVE & OTHER POEMS

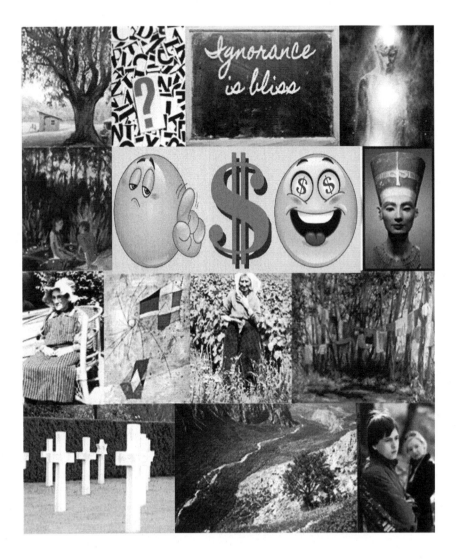

FIRST LOVE

When I was fifteen
I knew in every cell and
Atom of my being
What love was.
I knew it was painful,
Cloying, an unbearable sweetness,
A heavy weightlessness,
A hopeless, tangled mass of
Contradictions.

Oh, God, she was so beautiful,
All-perfect, and mine,
Yes, mine,
Except she barely spoke to me,
Too busy to linger and hear
My tongue-tied burblings or
Even my clownish attempts
To show her how clever I really was.
All that induced only deeper silences
Before she drifted over to Wally.

How could she even talk to him?
He was dolt personified,
Always smiling and most highly regarded
By everyone, by other dolts especially,
Although he, being most handsome,
Was king of the dolts,
And his magnetism drew them to him
Like helpless iron filings.
He was always central,
And with Nancy by his side,
My Nancy.

LOVE...?

Love is...?
I do not know.
Passion? Perhaps, until used up.
Simple devotion? Could be, if sustained,
I suppose, with ups and downs
In shares not necessarily equal.
An aching of the heart? For a while, yes.
Habit steady as a heartbeat?
A pragmatic possiblity surely.
Or is it all of these as well as
The indefinable years?

I opt for the last above
Because love may not be, cannot be,
Should not be defined,
Not even for a couple specified.
It is, well, it is a being,
A kaleidoscope, a mélange
Of shards that together try to tell it all
About being together day after day,

Moments fiery, moments calm,
Thousands upon thousands of them
Mostly forgettable and forgotten.

It is helping each other
Sometimes graciously, sometimes less so,
A being and a sharing and a doing
Each in his or her unique way
Until it's impossible to tell
Which is which and who is who.
Then it comes about:
Twenty-five, fifty, sixty years, more.
Love...?
I still do not know,
But I suspect it's so.

CEMETERY IN NORMANDY

Irony beyond comprehension,
This quiet and solemn expanse of graves
Extending beyond one's imagination,
Graves of boys, of men, so called,
Frightened and doing impossibilities,
Torn asunder, bleeding on the beach below,
Dying there in thunderous noise and in the sea,
Then placed here in ironic serenity,
Peaceful as a day in spring.

Whoever wasn't there can hardly know
What happened on the beach below.
These grounds I walk are most disturbing,
Perhaps their beauty, their serenity,
Unlike the hours when horror prevailed,
Makes these grounds so strange and sad,
This myriad of graves of the young,
Grounds now so calm, so sweet to stroll.
Thus it is wherever battles raged,
At all these burial sites that followed,

Visitors whisper, revere, ponder
Where vast numbers of the young
Killed and were killed for causes
Both noble and not.

So much to feel, so much to say,
Best let silence define the day.

OUT OF BODY

Suddenly came a pounding in his chest
Like nothing else he'd ever felt:
Hard and smashing, debilitating,
Pain like rocks hurtling at him
And none missing,
Pain like iron weights crushing him,
Everything aswirl and spinning
Round and round
With a blinding crash,
Then everything collapsing
Like him to the floor.

Gone, his heart was gone,
And he was dead, lying there until
A gleam, dark, with specks of light
Appeared, and within the gleam
He was very young again.
Then his father faded in,
Tall and straight and good, who said,
"It's all right, my boy, it's all right."

And he smiled as did the boy.
He felt so warm and comforted
That tears filled his eyes.

Then gone, all was gone,
But yet another pain as he lay
Trembling, convulsing,
A pain of burning on his chest
And on his side.
He opened his eyes to see
A person in uniform bending over,
Holding paddles and he knew
He hadn't died, not quite.
Instead he'd travelled very far,
Travelled to beyond, very far,
In a minute more or less.

Everyone who was tending him
Noticed on his face a smile.

REACHING

There are facts and there is truth,
And I suppose they sometimes coincide,
But still I'm not so sure
Which came first and maybe has to
(Chicken-egg conundrum).
I do know that most of us are, or were,
Reaching for truth somewhere out there.

Plato would no doubt have an answer
Of one sort or another,
Maybe no better than yours or mine,
But it's all quite significant, reaching,
Except that words can bully us,
Can tease, cajole and tease again
Until doubts flicker in our head.

Some surrender to them,
Others soldier on,
Some ridicule each dreamer,
Others wonder how they
Might try a reach or two themselves.

WHAT YOU DON'T KNOW

Ah, the fruits of ignorance, it seems to me,
Are far simpler than the concepts sophists posit
For those who need to know where and what is happiness.

Perhaps the lamb springing from the earth it loves,
Knowing not that his gentle shepherd will
Skewer him before two weeks,
Is happiness. Who knows?

The plump diner in his sixties, wallet and stomach full,
A sweet-breasted mistress attending to his every whim,
The fine Scotch he's drunk veiling him from himself,
Is happiness. I don't know, do you?

Or the lad doing deeds of goodness in the jungle,
Helping the festering village purify its water,
Not realizing that in the capital outside the jungle
Three whispering men are counting out
The countless pesos stolen to purchase the jungle,
Is happiness. It just might be, you know.

Or the mother who's just bathed her child,
Who'll die fifteen years hence in a most avoidable car collision;
The painter who's dabbed his final color on a painting
That will be burned as junk two decades hence;
And the long-distance runner fully unaware
That Lou Gehrig's will overtake him three years down the road.

There is yet another image,
One where she worked hard and followed the rules,
Never once believing or even hoping she'd make it,
Which strangely made her work harder still,
More stubborn and determined without knowing why,
And indeed she made it, praised by all,
Adored even unto the end of her many years
And never knowing her ignorance was a blessing.
This, too, might be happiness.

THE RICH AREN'T REALLY SO

The rich are just like you and me,
No doubt about it.
My rich friends suffer like the rest of us,
Maybe even more,
Because they have responsibilities we don't,
And there is about them, these friends,
Great dignity, nobility, for
They suffer in silence.

And that's why it's just as well
Our ethicists and such,
Empathizing with their wealthy patrons,
Remind us of a simple truth:
Rich or poor, doesn't matter one iota.
Health and happiness are where it's at;
All else is flimflam, nothing more's required.

Not only do these good folk preaching
Say it's so, my rich friends also do:
"Wealth does not bring happiness.
Believe me, I know,
Or joy or contentment or ease or
Serenity or equanimity or peace or
Fulfillment or satisfaction or true comfort.
You're just as well off without it.
Really, I know all about wealth.
Not what it's cracked up to be."

Maybe, but it does help, doesn't it?

RETIREMENT HOME

The people here are quite diversified,
Some stand straight and tall,
Others are melacholy exemplars of disrepair,
Many have canes and walkers
And wheel chairs and care-givers.
Still they are a hearty lot
Defying the undefiables,
Much of it no doubt bravado.

Especially do I notice one, a lady,
Her face a cartographer's parchment,
Her eyes steady as she stares ahead.
Upon that face is etched:
Pain, love, sadness, defiance, acceptance,
Years beyond remembering,
Moments vanished forever.
Only expectation is lacking.

She is alive but truly ancient,
With her antique bonnet and her brooch,
Her dress, everything from long ago
That her children, themselves now old,

Brought to her at her insistence.
She would persist for a brief forever,
Having already spanned decades
From the origin of her bonnet
To modern medical ministrations,
Surviving beyond a century
And still able on occasion
To gift you with a smile
As sweet and simple as her life
Has not been,
And even to whisper a word or two.

Although I return her smile,
I keep thinking to myself,
My God, how very old she is
And looks her age,
Every single day of it.
How strange I can only think of her
As very, very old and of myself,
Well, as young, but if that is so
Then what am I doing in this place
Where so many hobble here and there?
But then I am comforted,
For at least I am aware, conscious,
Able to analyze my state,
And know that I know
That I am here and certainly far removed
From that antique soul who sits in her chair.

Yes, I feel better until I return to where I live
And for some reason glance into the mirror,
Which, though I argue well in counteraction,
Insists on sharing with me its truth.
And then, harking up the antique lady,
I see perhaps she might not be
So very old after all.

I AM NINETY-TWO

Biking one day through French countryside,
To escape a bit the August heat,
I stopped beneath a friendly tree
Next to a vineyard ripening apace.

Standing close beside the road,
With shears held firmly in her hand
Protective cloth upon her head,
Dressed late 19th century,
An old lady working there
Smiled warmly as she waved.
Few teeth, alas, complemented her grin.

"Monsieur," said she, pride in her voice,
"J'ai quatre-vignt-douze ans."[1]
Then she snapped her shears, click-click,
Flashing her grin again at me.
"Moi," said I, "j'ai seulement trente-six."[2]

"Ah, poor baby," she replied,
"You have much to learn."
"That's true, but I have lots of hope."
"What a pity, such foolishness, don't bother,
Waste of time, my lad, just be,
And you'll get by, believe me."

We said goodbye, I hopped my bike
And pedaled down the road,
Feeling uneasy as I thought,
Maybe wisdom's not all it's cracked up to be,
But then again, there she stood
With pruning shears tending grapes joyfully
On a hot August day,
Ninety years plus and no doubt some to go.

I sped down a hill faster than was wise,
Wondering why I was doing what I did
And trying hard not to hope or see ahead.

[1] "J'ai quatre-vingt-douze ans." - "I am 92."
[2] "Moi, j'ai seulement trente-six." - "Me, I'm only 36."

HANGING OUT THE CLOTHES

A sunny day at last,
And so how very nice
To hang out all the clothes
To aromatize them all
With April breezes
And a cooperating sun,
To scour them of germs
And who knows what other
Evils that have been hiding
In our closet and even
In the electric dryer
Winter requires we use?

There they are laboriously
Strung across the line:
Bras and pants and shirts
And handkerchiefs and socks,
Pajamas, too, along with slips
And blouses and assorted towels.
What a rainbow of woven stuff
Fluttering, flapping,

With an occasional clapping of
Flags of many nations,
A spectrum of worlds
Waving in friendly rhythms
To inspire the little boy
To dash beneath the
Animation of his mother's
Hygienic ministrations
On a lovely day in spring.

Back and forth he runs,
Our little boy of three,
With an occasional whoop
Of joy over the mystery of
Running back and forth
Beneath so many flapping
Colors there for him alone,
And then just beyond
Trees beckon too
In competition with all
That undulating color.
What to do, what to do?
The little boy thinks.
A decision must be made.
A run to the trees or
Again beneath the colors,
But it matters not at all,
At least for now,
Because Mother is calling
The little boy to lunch,
And so trees and banners
Will have to wait
Until the little boy comes back.

BEFORE THE STORM

Just before the storm came rumbling and tumbling in,
If a tourist were fortunate and hosted by a friendly magic,
There before such a visitor, invisible to the participants,
Lay a scene too perfect even for artists who do calendars,
With a maple giant all gnarled from countless decades
And a grassy meadow beyond where two children played
In sunlight as warm and gentle as a mystical blessing,
While awash in shade poured generously from the tree
An aged woman sat, also gnarled by many years,
Great-grandma to those children not so far away,
All, everything and everyone, in natural harmony,
Perfection of a moment forever distilled so deep
Within the memories of the participants
They will have great difficulty remembering it, if at all,
Except perhaps in some final moments of their lives,
All too beautiful for ordinary recall,
So ordinary such breathless beauty and perfection,
A monarch emerging from its chrysalis,
And except in future repetition it is not permanent
And so that storm that came rumbling and tumbling in

Suddenly, almost mockingly, introduced yin and yang
When its thunderous kettle drums turned silence
Into rhythmic cacophony and its flashes stabbed
Into that meadow lit golden but moments ago.

Our little cast, children and great-grandma,
Proved how remarkably people, granted the occasion,
Can move through space to somewhere else,
As they all did, to the little shed where Father
Kept his mower and other beloved tools of his.
Laughing, yet breathless, they all clung together,
Two vastly separated generations who yet could share
That moment of comparison between
Two worlds, that of sun and laughter,
Of dark and laughter and each
A special difference and each a part of the other.
It all somehow, the storm and all that went before,
Seemed perfect, the way things ought to be.

NEFERTITI

Lovely Queen, you are dead.
Like the slightest of forgotten things you are gone,
Like melted snows and jackal yells,
You who owned the endless shifting sands
And thought all time a mere jewel upon your throat.

You are dead, Haughty Queen,
Like your king and the slaves that carved his tomb.
Still you almost smile at those who call you dead.

But you are dead, Vain Queen,
And all your sighing palms
And once-dreamed dreams of self
And unseen snake crushed by your procession.

Yet, oh yet, my Calm, Sweet, Lovely Queen,
You gaze forever at time itself,
But I am certain you once died
There beside the River Nile.

KOSTAS

Kostas held the same street corner seven days a week.
Like him, his flowers leaned in their paper cones
Against a grimy building fifty times his height.
His shoulders sagged beneath the humid air
And a thousand unkind years.
His face was dark and stubbly, remote.
Often his friend Yorghos passed to tell him news of home:
Of his angry brother in the colonels' jail[1] -
The horophilaki[2] had been looking for their chance,
Of his widowed sister cleaning floors in a hotel by the sea,
Of their friends encumbered by the thousand unkind years
And the colonels' Greece.

Their bit of land by the sea was gone,
Taken by the rulers for their officers' homes.
The little money paid them vanished quickly
Into the pockets of their creditors and the ticket agent.
Now he was a man without a home,
A man with flowers on a corner in Chicago.
But Greece was home and Greece was memories:
Blue-green mountains, rocky beaches by a deep blue sea,

Sounds that donkeys make along their stony paths,
Smell of grapes in the bee-watched autumn press,
Flickering olive leaves for cool rests from the sun,
Brassy goats and solemn sheep on lonely hills,
The tinkling bouzouki[3], the smoky taverna, the tang of retsina[4].

How good it might be
If only the important men would leave half a chance,
But did they ever?
A man musn't be thought a thing and a man must eat;
A man mustn't live frightened and debased;
He mustn't live a prisoner in his land.
So what was left but memories?

Once he'd helped Yorghos move some goods to the west.
They stopped the truck by Delphi[5], which he had never seen;
They stood by the road below the sun-struck Phaedriades[6]
Above the Valley of the Pleistos[7],
So deep and full of space that its million olive trees
Were like moss by a forest stream.
An eagle swept before them, a dark visible breeze.
Kostas looked up to see another sailing fast
Just this side of the intense October sky,
And longed to touch him, and his soul succeeded:
He looked down upon himself and Yorghos,
Down upon the great Phaedriades and the places of the gods,

Down and down into the mossy valley.
For a moment Kostas knew joy more keen than pain.
A timid lady approached to choose a cone of roses;
She expected at least a commercial smile from Kostas,
But there was only his remote and silent look.
Stupid or maybe dangerous, she thought,
And stepped away without the roses.
How was she to know that he was watching eagles over Delphi?

[1] colonels' jail - In 1967 fascist military officers overthrew the democratically elected Greek government.
[2] horophilaki - Greek gendarmerie.
[3] bouzouki - Greek stringed instrument similar to the mandolin or banjo.
[4] retsina - Resinated white wine.
[5] Delphi - Spectacular site of ancient Greek ruins relevant principally to Apollo and the Delphic Oracle.
[6] Phaedriades - Great cliffs rising behind Delphi.
[7] Valley of the Pleistos - The Valley of the Pleistos River below Delphi is packed with olive trees.

SONNET FOR THE REST OF US

Poets there are who speak in tongues unknown
Except to those of such linguistic bent
Their wisdom is their true testosterone,
And God help those who're not so cognisant
As they who praise the dense obscurity
Of poets who shun the melancholy fate
Of being grasped by mundane entities,
An end no cryptic poet can contemplate.

There once was such a one, a baffling poet
Well praised by cognoscenti everywhere,
Who, drunk one night and briefly profligate,
Penned simple lines as light as autumn air.
Next morn he rose with pounding head and learned
His fame was gone: he had become discerned.

FAMILY & RECOLLECTION

GHOSTS

A photograph, perhaps, is best of all
To bring back moments lost from long ago,
But then that tune you suddenly recall
Invades your mind, invades your soul, and so
You play it once again and then again
Until through windows opened to the spring
The lilac's luscious scent comes drifting in,
And other ghosts glide swiftly on the wing.

A view, a sound, a scent, a touch, a taste,
It matters not the key that opens doors
As long as you are willing to embrace
Those many ghosts that are uniquely yours.
However they appear, remember, too,
That they are, heart and soul, a part of you.

A MODEST IMMORTALITY

About heaven and hell, I know little,
And as to immortality nothing at all,
But I do welcome my special ghosts,
The ones we all possess,
Who might visit us unbidden
Through simple means.

For instance,
When celery grows a little limp,
My wife sets it in the fridge
In cold water in a bowl
And adds a touch of salt.
Every single time it works,
And voilà, the celery's firm again.

"Neat trick," I say admiringly.
She smiles before she says,
"Your mother taught me that
Almost before I didn't know
Boiling water wasn't hard to do."

Strange, for at that moment
I saw and heard my mother, long gone,
Standing before me and looking pleased,
And so I saw and heard her once again,
Immortal for an unexpected moment
And as long as I shall live.

MYSTERY

Whatever happened to cool dark barns,
Where frantic motes of dust scurried to the sun
And hay smelled so delicious
You envied the cows below the loft?

What has replaced the shaded spring house,
Haunt of the delicate crayfish and other sweet enigmas,
Place to cleanse and cool the carrot pulled from near the door
And tasting of earth and summer?

Even the hill for flying kites is gone,
Along with the spring sunset tasted by kite and flier,
And the river that offered the many challenges, gone,
And the hidden mountain path that led to somewhere.

All gone, and the child
Who won't return.

GRANDMA'S CANARY

Grandma's canary was really nothing special to see,
Just an ordinary little yellowish thing,
But oh how he could sing!
Billy's trill could penetrate your ear and,
Whether you wanted to or not, you listened.
Maybe he was hoping against all odds
That somewhere little Millie Canary might hear him
And come flying right into his love nest.
This never happened, but he never stopped his song,
Especially when Grandma hove to
And sent him a loving kiss through pursed lips.
They really did like each other, two kindred souls,
Because she sang, too, lah-de-dahing ditties
From her hard childhood long since gone,
Although her voice was so soft you could barely hear
Her little lilting melodies.
Billy and Grandma communicated, the two of them,
Athough none of us knew what they were saying.

It was always this way
Until that certain day in spring when Grandma
Came to Billy's cage and gently loosed his door.
Just then a car horn sounded through the open window,
And Billy, instead of lighting on Grandma's finger,
Flicked almost invisibly out the cage.
Then out he flew, a yellow splash, out an open window
Into unending space toward the nearby maple.
Quickly, remarkably so, cage in hand,
Grandma dashed outside to the trunk of the maple tree.
She spotted Billy perched on a twig high up.
She called to him, she sent him her melodies,
And for a moment he listened, his head cocked toward her.
She hoisted his cage toward him as far as arms could stretch,
Hoping its open door would entice him to return.
He looked down once, then said goodbye with a tiny chirp
Before he sprang from his twig, fluttered through a leafy break
And was in an instant gone,
For a second or so a spot, then a dot of color below the sky
Before he was no more.

Grandma turned away, not crying,
But I never heard her sing again.

RAPHAEL'S CORNER

For him it was a world quite adequate,
A simple corner of a living room,
A space familiar as each breath you take
And where when evening came he could resume
The occupation of his small domain,
Where he could sit and read and contemplate
And search for visions lost he might regain,
Which youth in him might somehow activate.

How wonderful if each and every one
Of us could find a special corner where
We might just find our lives have but begun
If gazing deep into ourselves we swear
To strive to know just what we were at best
And seize those youthful dreams we once caressed.

GRANDCHILD

It isn't hard for me to say
What wins the prize on any day.
I realize that there are those
Who disagree and would impose
The prize they swear's the best by far,
Their undisputed exemplar.

Some swear that mountains win the test
While others say the ocean's best,
Or advocate the sun and moon,
Competitors quite opportune,
And others still advance the sky,
Whatever's grand and very high.

However, still what I endorse
Is choice so evident of course
That even those who disagree
Will surely somehow have to see
Their claims must all be reconciled
To what is peerless, my grandchild.

VISIT TO AN EMPTY SPACE

How strange it is to visit where you lived
To find your home, your life's essential core,
All vanished, gone, and not to be retrieved,
As though you never dwelled right here before.
The space where stood your home is nothing now
But excavation waiting for the frame
To make the concrete walls that will allow
Completion of a new commercial same.

What right have I to disapprove of this?
(The only claim I have is it was here
I lived and even learned to reminisce.)
At least I've memory to commandeer,
For all I gained in searching for my past
Is learning it alone is what can last.

PROOF OF GRAVITY

Watching clouds move
Like herds of fluffy elephants
Across deep blue pastures and
Of course birds doing all the things
Birds do, like dipping, soaring,
Banking, diving, and in brief
Simply flying by flapping wings
Or holding steady on invisible air,
I knew I, too, must fly.

Eight year olds can be inventive
Should need arrive, as it often does,
And I had a need to fly more than
Attending school or taking out the trash
Or sleeping or eating or anything.
What to do, what to do?
And so I did, involving one who
Hadn't a clue that she would be
A part of my empirical act to be,

My poor grandmother, innocent
Of everything except innocence.
No one was around that day,
And it being summertime
School was not imprisoning me.
Mother, Dad, both out working,
Older brother some place else,
Most likely up to no good.
And so to Grandmother's dresser,
A quick search through each drawer
Until there before my eyes
Lay what I was looking for.
She being from out the past,
Her silky slip was very long,
Hanging down to the floor,
A garment suitable for one
Who'd emulate the denizens
Of the invisible air.
Removing it, I quickly rearranged
Her garments so as to conceal
What had been done.

On to Grandma's sewing basket
And its gigantic scissors.
Kneeling on the floor, I thoroughly
Destroyed her undergarment,
Rendering it into a silken square.
Then came next the heavy cord,
Eight lengths of which I clipped
Quite evenly, proud of my progress.
A cord tied tight and very well

At every corner and in between
Until I arrived at nothing less
Than a viable parachute
To carry me through invisible air.

I dragged it all about,
Yanking sharply on the cords
To provide the needed proof
That all would hold as
I wholeheartedly intended.
It did indeed pass muster
And even almost looked
Like what it was supposed to be,
If you cocked your head a certain way,
Except, of course, that parachutes
Are usually round,
Along with other attributes.
But never mind, don't judge
A book by its cover.
My parachute was exactly that,
A parachute central to my plan.
Hadn't I frequently
Tied string to handkerchief,
Supplied a weight and tossed it high
To watch it float gently down.
I was soon to do the very same,
With me as tied-on weight.

Heart pounding, I ran to a window
Letting onto the lower roof,
My chute bunched up awaiting
Its service to one in need.
I crawled through the open window
Until I was fully on the roof,
Feeling confident and agile
As I gazed to the roofs higher yet.
I climbed easily along the slope
That took me to roof number two,
Paused a few brief moments
Before proceeding higher still,
Slightly breathless now but
Heart remarkably steady
Beneath the weight of determination.
Steeper still the final passage
That would bring me up above
To roof three just below the sky.

There at last, the pinnacle,
The summit, the apex of my dream,
The sharp gable of our house
Beyond which nothing more than space,
Which I was about to conquer.
Carefully, cautiously I walked
The sharp ridge toward its end
High above the ground,
Holding tight to my balled-up device.
Reaching my destination at the edge,
I stood to my full height
And unfurled my parachute,
Wrapping well about one wrist

The ends of all eight cords.
I gazed down and down,
And it all did seem a bit far away,
But never mind, I thought,
This is the moment I intended.
I drew in deep breaths,
Glanced down once again,
Then sprang way far off
Into invisible air.
Two seconds? Less?
I'll never know how fast I dropped
Until I struck.

The doctor shook his head a bit
Before declaring my concussion
Was not so serious as it could have been:
The bush had eased my fall.
"He'll have to stay in bed," said he,
Words I did not want to hear.
There were other things I had to do,
Things that shouldn't have to wait before
Summer's end and my annual captivity.

My brother, though, looked down
On me most scornfully and said,
Showing off his worldly wisdom,
"So you and Sir Isaac Newton
Are one and the same, are you?
His apple didn't fall up either,
And you, you dope, did you?"
I gladly would have killed him
If my head didn't hurt so much.

FIRST SOLO

My instructor called over the engine's voice,
"Taxi over there and throttle back."
I did, and as soon as we sat still in the grass,
Prop visible as it slowly turned in sync
To the engine's metronomic tick,
He said, "You're ready, take her up."
Then removing himself from the tiny craft,
He called out, "Three times around. Good luck."
And he was gone and I was alone,
Thinking how uncomfortable it was to see his stick
Moving about to my command with him not there.

Throttle and left rudder advanced a bit and we,
Ship and I, bumped from grass to tarmac.
Odd how at that moment so very much
Flooded through my every sense:
The engine's hoarse hum,
My sweaty grip on the stick,
The pleasant aroma of gas,
And blue mountains far removed.

I remembered then what I must do
To guarantee my craft was right and ready:
A check of ailerons, rudder, elevator, brakes,
A final test of the engine.
Again a push forward on the throttle
And a turn onto the runway,
Then all the way with the throttle
Followed by the engine's one high note
And a steady roll forward, ever faster,
And a bit forward with the stick
And the lift behind of the tail
And then slowly back with the stick,
And I knew exactly when wheels
No longer touched the ground,
Smooth as water on a windless lake,
A quick moment when I lost my breath
And swallowed deep.

We lifted up, plane and I, to altitude,
Feeling light and bouncy on the air,
And then left on stick and rudder
To begin creation of
My aerial box around the field.
Again and once again I banked and turned
Until I had the runway straight before me
And the signal from the tower,
The light gun flashing green,
Telling me to land.
Concentration told me what to do,
Fully conscious, nothing automatic,
That happy achievement for the future.

A welcoming possibility the runway as
I began to throttle back and then
Push gently forward a little on the stick.
Back more with the throttle, gently,
And I was just a few feet above
Where I was supposed to be.
Then full off with the throttle,
A stretch of floating parallel
With the welcoming strip,
Then back on the stick,
Followed by a little squeal of rubber tires
To announce my three-point set-down,
But I bounced a bit, then stayed
Where I was supposed to,
Except there were two more times around.
Again I forwarded the throttle
And lifted up the tail
To fly my required repetition,
But still it was like the first time,
Unique and incredibly grand.

Again alone in space, my little craft and I
Began to bask in the utopian moment
Of a lovely world being all ours.
Looking down upon its Lilliputian design,
I felt I was obligated, yes I,
To bless or pity it all,
Tiny people, tiny cars, everything.
Then of course a matter
Merely of seconds more before
I was cleared to land again,
Then off again for my final pattern, the third,
And acceptance as a pilot, of sorts.
All over too quickly, so much so
I hardly noticed my final bounce
That denoted another mediocre landing,
Because, after all, I had done it,
I had been in space all alone.
No one, not a single soul was there
Watching me navigate an invisible sea,
While doing so I was commandant
Of my world and me.

THE GREAT DEPRESSION

We had a garage, but it was long empty,
Bereft of auto, like the many pots bereft of chickens
Despite election ads promising otherwise.
Yes, empty our garage except at night
When on its concrete floor a half dozen people
Leaping from the N&W cargo trains
Pounding the tracks behind our home
Hunkered down for shelter
Before moving on to everywhere.
If the weather proved half decent,
Some would visit the river nearby
To scrub away their travel grime.
Mostly men, but sometimes a woman, too,
Or a young lad travelling with his father,
Carrying balled-up sack or worn valise,
Whatever little they might possess.

We were poor, very poor, but hungry-poor?
No, we always ate quite sufficiently,
Beans and simple stuff

While steaks and other luxuries were
As invisible as the car in our garage.
Then almost every morning a ritual occurred
Just after Dad left early for his store
Before Mother joined him, a dedication
Made by her and her mother, my grandmother,
A sandwich-making time, busy moments
When the two, with children helping some,
Slathered their healthful, homemade spreads
Until a neat and sizable stack of sandwiches
Sat next to the apples on a platter,
Not to mention the pitcher of lemonade.
We kids then delivered the sustenance to our porch,
Where we knew the hungry would come.

Word somehow travelled fast back then,
Necessity being invention's mother.
I recall the marks done in chalk where our
Walkway began, clear X's meaning food was here.
However, some people far better off than we,
Others much like us and thus close to the margin,
Had unkind words to designate the itinerants:
Tramps, bums, derelicts, deadbeats, vagabonds,
Hobo being one of the nicer terms.
They resented and cursed the wanderers
Who might harm them, steal their jobs
Or, being too lazy to work, indulge in poverty.
But those of such unpleasant view were far fewer
Than the others who offered comfort and relief,
Who, rich or poor, had well imbibed the mantra,
"There but for the Grace of God go I."
My mother and my grandmother were not exceptional.

Many more today denigrate the poor,
Condemning them for their deficiencies,
For their laziness, their love of welfare
That provides them with such benefits
That welfare queens and kings live high
While laughing at their benefactors,
The doers and the makers maintaining them.
I also learn about the children in our land
Who go to sleep each night hungry and deprived.
Their numbers are vast.
I am aware, too, of other numbers just as vast,
Of righteous politicians and like-minded citizens
Inveighing against the poor and their children
In the name of God, frugality, and profits for some,
Loathing any governmental help for the poor,
Cutting programs that might snatch away the poor
From an abyss of nothingness,
Because such help, after all, is not unlike stealing
From the doers and the makers and the wealth of our land,
A process our nation can ill afford when
The churches can do what's necessary.

Hearing the cries of the suffering burden-bearers
Unjustly forced to commit kindness,
I remember my mother and her mother
And other mothers throughout our town
Making sandwiches for people they did not know.

FAREWELL TO NEW YORK

We left our city, this time for good,
Lifting off from LaGuardia,
Then turning left below the clouds
For our final view:
The Hudson, gleaming in the sun,
Its famous bridge but a seeming inch or two
This side of Grant's Tomb
And farther south another glimpse,
Now of the Empire State,
Pointing its own pathway to the sky.
And that was all that was left
Of the place we had long called home.

We were flying southward now and soon
Lifted through dank clouds
Into blinding sunlight and endless space,
Wondering if it would be fun
To trampoline across the fluff below.
An easy flight to our destination,
In a sense too easy for people leaving

But who knew that New York City
Daily made no bones about it:
"I am for the young, the rich, the striving."

We tried a while to contest our city's truth,
But lost the match,
And so now we are 500 miles away,
Measured arrow-straight and hard to accept,
It going all too quickly for ordinary grasp.

We settled in after jousts with weather,
Jousts with movers, jousts with ourselves,
Until the last box was unpacked
And we painfully discovered
What had been lost and what, unfortunately,
Had not been lost, seeing we had overpacked.
A month or two after moving's trauma,
A mini-hell you would consider
Not conferring even on an enemy,
We began seriously our exploring,
Sniffing here and sniffing there
Rather like dogs addicted to lamposts.
It was all, to say the least,
Somewhat different from New York,
And soon we wearied of the questions
Posed to us for reasons ranging
From the sincere to soporific politeness.

Among the questions were the obvious ones:
Do you miss the subways and the buildings?
You miss the delis and the shows?
In brief, all the expected et ceteras,
And the answer is of course a simple yes.
So what's new?

Well, what's new other than the obvious
Is the sky, the one of our flight,
Much like the one found right here.
It took us a while to realize
That when we emerged into the night
It was a dark so vast and palpable
It pressed upon us, weightlessly so,
Vast space, vast darkness,
Making us feel small beneath a galactic dome,
Except at times when moon and stars
Shone brilliantly upon us,
And even so space beyond words remained.
Otherwise, profound blackness, informing us
That, yes, it was indeed nighttime,
Just as the deep blue vastness by day
Helped transport us into infinite space.
All a rediscovery, the moon and stars
And infinite space both day and night,
A revelation to know they were really there,
Not just in a planetarium or magazine.

Here at last was the difference
Beyond the obvious and the foolish.
Like Hamlet we had in the City been
Bounded in a nutshell
Beneath another kind of dome
As high perhaps as only the highest building.
No sky beyond to speak of, nor cloud nor star,
If not invisible, then insignificant.
But then within that finite dome
Where night and day hardly competed,
Bright lights and sunshine blending symbiotically,
It was for us grand enough,
Bound only by human limitations,
And not the impossibilities of the truly infinite.
It was comfortable, truth to tell, and it was we
Who felt grander than a space
Too vast to peer beyond might allow,
So that within our smaller, man-made dome
We felt ourselves quite infinite.

We won't bother to explain this to our friends.

GOODBYE, A CRITIQUE

Goodbyes can be terrible.
There's that first-time separation
When homesickness weighs
So heavy on your heart
Each aching breath reminds you
That you endure a loss
Almost too much to endure,
Which only time can comfort,
And so you long for time to pass.
It does and you breathe again
And begin to live again.
With time and enough goodbyes
You form a soothing habit,
A certain hardness, a disdain
Of feelings so tender
You were embarrassed,
So that never again
Will you be rendered helpless.

But then of course there are
Goodbyes that fly quickly past:
Everyday, common ones,
When you say to mate or friend
Goodbye, whom you'll be seeing
A few hours later in the day.
Perhaps better if you'd said
So long or au revoir or, dramatically,
Till we meet again,
As of course you will, and soon.

Some goodbyes might even comfort
Like the one that time
You said with heartfelt relief
As you waved to relatives
Who had overstayed their visit.
However, then, a surge of guilt
That you had felt that way
Dissipated your relief,
So much so that even as you waved
You called out, "Come again soon!"

There is yet a last goodbye,
Perhaps whispered,
More likely mute, unuttered,
But felt and thought and felt again,
Future's inescapable invention
Planned for tomorrow or decades hence.
Sometimes it provides relief
For traveler and survivor alike,
But always it is final, the end,
A boundary impassable
We try to comprehend,
And that last unheard goodbye
Is about the best that we can do.

VISIT TO DELOS[1]

Lizards and visitors know Delos well,
Although lizards, being mostly silent,
Are probably wiser about it all.
Happily you see them everywhere.
Just when you think the island's complexity
Has nothing more to confuse you with,
An interesting fleck of muscled color occurs,
Pauses a second to be identified,
Then snaps below another stone
Where you would swear a knife blade couldn't go.

Another flick, just past your feet,
A flexible twist of speed,
And you've glimpsed at your feet
A head far older than these iconic ruins,
Far older than these eroded lions,
Than history itself,
Whose eyes say to you,
"Fool" or "Hello, Brother," or
"Better luck in your next reincarnation."

Then your little friend is gone,
So with a sigh you continue to investigate,
Not yourself, mind, but the ruins of Delos,
Same as the multitudes checking off the obligations
Named by your guide of many tongues and jokes.
At least an hour before your boat to Mykonos[2],
When you hardly know, or care, whether
The present stone intricacy before you half a meter high
Is the Hypostyle Hall or the Portico of Antigonos
Or the South Agora or even the god's temple itself,
When you've sunk beneath Apollo's burning gaze,
Your friend, or his brother, again scampers past
In rapid pursuit of you know not what.

You feel distracted, saved, by this living thing,
And he, shiny-eyed, dart-tongued,
Gray, greenish black and lithe, does not disappoint you,
For this time, perhaps with tasty insects aplenty,
He appears again and again,
And you bless him for his simple dignity,
For his secret purposes, his charming swiftness,
His being, his knowing what it's all about
And what must be done: life with purpose.
He makes me think, I envy him.
He is significant, mysterious, amusing.
I love him for ever dwelling here with Apollo,
A living thing closer to the god, no doubt,
Than any of us intruders.

It was then, here where Leto bore her golden son,
That Apollo, Healer, God of Light, God of Knowledge,
Approving of my new-found wisdom,
Smiled.

[1] Delos - Greek Cycladic island, mythological birthplace of Apollo
and his sister Artemis.
[2] Mykonos - Another Greek Cycladic island close to Delos.

(On a secret visit to the Acropolis of Mycenae before and during sunrise)

MYCENAE[1] AT DAWN

Having scaled the fence like the best of committed thieves,
We walked, or rather glided, harmonious, yet alien,
   insubstantial,
Through the Gate of Lions,
Through chill alleys wrapped in the star-dotted dark,
Into tense and eerie moments we felt we too had experienced.
We could not see in the dark the Gate, but knew well
That two lions, rampant, headless,
Poised frozen above us in rigid denial of millennia,
Two great lions heavier than silence and graceful as space.

Within we trod the stone and earthen ramp,
Black but for an almost trace of light
Like tunes not quite remembered,
In the starlit indigo chill of an aging night
Past the royal pit of graves
Of kings asleep long before other sleeping kings,

An abyss now filled with dark emptiness and seeming,
Once bearer of gold pressed on shattered skulls and
    powdered bones,
Of glorified might all lost in common ends.

Up the ramp toward a sky inching toward a lighter tint,
Up steps irregularly smooth that certain feet had known
Other than Schliemann's and ours and a Mrs. Smith's of
    Witchita Falls,
Into the royal palace where,
More felt than seen, Mount Zara² pressed upon us
Frozen like those lions and as tense and mighty as a bull
    restrained.

We stood a little breathless from fear or awe or even
    unaccustomed exercise,
Or yet some unnamed mystery regarding chill bronze
    ghosts at dawn,
Within the throne room the archaeologists have so named,
Certainly within the palace of kings,
Especially one too proud, too arrogant, too cruel,
Doomed, cursed, slain, and, above all, sung
Through the ages by a visionary blind man and by writers
    of plays.

In a night chilled further by dawn's thin breeze,
Awash in swift, chaotic meanings,
We watched night bend over her infant day.
We stood alone with Homer and Aeschylus³ and
    Agamemnon and knew

That here Clytemnestra and her sulking Aegisthus killed,
She mother of Iphigenia slain by her child's own father,
Her husband, who thus here fell, king of all the Greeks,
Sinking like the last of flaming Troy into his own bloody destiny.

Now Zara, visible brooding triangle, yet haloed into
    something softer,
Grew gray, grew blue, grew touched with morning gold,
With colors that pursued our dreams,
Poor frantic owls refusing to surrender,
From light to the pregnant darkness of that pit below,
To the final home of ancestors of
Justly murdered king and justly slaughtered queen.

Could it be that hesitating Orestes and shrill Electra,
Both bow-string taut, whispering here at dawn,
Had also sensed the same silent images,
Elusive hints that were all the future might allow?
Except for cursed Cassandra[4] whose omniscience
    mattered not.
Maddening, too, the gods give us hindsight, that cruel gift,
Once the future and now but frozen reduction.

Perhaps it was inevitable, then, that before a benign sun
Turned Zara into Grecian hill
And purple lakes into tended fields
We recognized our brother and our sister,
Those royal children,
Dead so long but unable to evade our trespass

Upon their secrets and their terrible actions,
Their cries, their crimes, their hideous obligations,
Their stumblings from bloody corridors to the Rock of Ares[5]
Where the Furies[6] would pretend to be satisfied.

Day was at last definite:
The illusion was gone and only ruins, vestiges, remained
For the diggers and the cataloguers, the guards, the tourists.
And so now warming to the friendly day,
We moved quickly from tumbled walls to ramp and then
Beyond the Gate of Lions
To a world where breakfast waited and
There was no blind poet to see our own little tale and sing it
So that empty places ages hence would teem for moments
With possibilities before dawn.

---

[1] Mycenae - Important Greek Bronze Age archaeological site known best for its acropolis and palace associated with such tragic names in Homeric and dramatic Greek literature as Agamemnon, Clytemnestra, Electra, Orestes, Cassandra. Henrik Schliemann, often called the father of modern archaeology, made important discoveries here and in ancient Troy.
[2] Mount Zara - Stands behind and close by the Acropolis of Mycenae.
[3] Aeschylus - Early Greek playwright best known for his tragedies dealing with Agamemnon, his wife Clytemnestra who killed him with the help of her lover Aegisthus, and their avenging children Electra and Orestes.
[4] Cassandra - Daughter of the Trojan king, given the gift of true prophecy, but then god-cursed so that no one would believe her.
[5] Rock of Ares - A large rock outcrop, the Areopagus, associated with justice, lies next to the Athenian Acropolis.
[6] Furies - Female Greek deities of vengeance.

AMIMALS

OUR CAT

Our cat pounces on sunlight when a splash of it appears,
Courtesy of leaves prancing outside the window,
And on moonbeams, too - same thing.

Stalking across the hospitable carpet,
Pounce, scratch, pounce in pursuit of
Balletic, invisible, immortal mice,
Our cat, ever the profound optimist,
Pounce, scratch, et cetera,
Bravely refuses to succumb to fantasy's reality.

All this after, in contorted comfort,
He had fallen asleep on the dining table
After scaling the drapery clear up to the ceiling
In search of windmills.

We of course talk to him about it all.
He listens, silent and unblinking,
Understanding every single word we speak
Without giving a feline's damn.

In order to cover our ignorance,
We blame him for his weirdness,
And he really is, you know, weird.
He is a cat, our cat.

EFBEE THE MYSTERIOUS

Cats like looking out of windows.
Our Efbee, Furball, most surely does:
Birds passing deliciously mere feet away
Or the neighbor's hateful dog off his leash.
But there are other times when he's there
For no valid reason that we know.
We decide to investigate,
So we sneak outside and hide in the bushes
In order to peer at Efbee's eyes because
The eyes of cats, God knows, can say a lot.
We study Efbee staring through his window.
He is gazing hypnotized, jealous maybe,
At a flock of seabirds soaring very high,
And, wonder of wonders, upon Efbee's face,
And certainly as well as in his eyes,
We sense something different there.

Those birds he is watching seem not to inspire
His usual hunger and intent to assassinate;
No tense twitching, no hungry drooling.
Instead, that look of his into the distant sky,
So available to that lucky flock of rising birds,
Tells of space, vast distances and, yes, dreams.
Now we believe that Efbee might be a dreamer
Who has come to realize, Efbee, like us, too,
That an horizon might be even better
Than food upon the wing,
And who knows, really,
What lies on the other side?

TROPICAL FISH, A BRIEF SAGA

They're a royal pain, tropical fish,
Unless you go for belly-ups
And other inevitabilities.
I once fulfilled my foolish wish,
Perhaps being in my cups
And lacking basic sensibilities.

Off we went, my wife and I,
She no less foolish than her spouse,
To a pet store teeming with animals
Intended to catch a sucker's eye:
Hamster, snake, fish, and mouse,
The exotic and the banal.

'Twas then our über moment came
When we entered that part of the store
Where swam many an impressive fish,
A who's who of tropicals by name:
Black Mollies, Bettas, Angels galore,
Gouramis, Swordtails, name your wish.

Screams of delight assailed our ears
When the three kids studied the plastic bags
Containing our finny, flitting rainbows.
Each plop of fish was met with cheers
And when some behaved like scalawags,
The children loudly clapped their kudos.

We watched our fish investigate
Their unclouded world of plants and rocks,
Even a pirate's sunken treasure chest,
Then laid out rules to feed and medicate,
Everything done quite orthodox.
As parents we felt good, we felt blessed.

We ignored our weatherman's overkill -
Che sarà, sarà, that sort of thing -
And so off to bed all five of us,
Comfy in the slight September chill,
Until just before the light of morning
We awoke to a frigid awfulness.

"The fish!" screamed our youngest tot.
A weird crew, all blanket-cloaked,
We raced to where the aquarium sat.
The heater is what we'd all forgot!
Our fish could well be croaked,
A matter of the thermostat.

Our aquatic menagerie remained afloat,
But not through effort of their own.
Propelled by circulating device,
They wafted through the yuck by rote,
Bellies exposed that dully shone,
Others drifting on their sides.

By dawn's light we then conferred
As to disposal of the little corpses.
I proposed burial at toilet,
A grave mistake, so I deferred.
Thus so it was beneath the birches
We buried all in one tiny basket.

We slumped back into the living room,
Now wonderfully warm, belatedly,
And took our several seats,
All eyes avoiding that tank of doom,
When suddenly our eldest called out ringingly,
"Guys, what do we know about parakeets?"

BACKYARD NOCTURNE

We built in our backyard a lily pond
To top our swanky neighbors with a show
Of waterfall and fish we hoped would spawn,
With lights a part of our scenario.
The night arrived to test our artistry:
The sound and light and waterfall switched on,
I turned my back and called for all to see,
Then looked again with pride on what we'd done.

How best describe my being traumatized?
A raccoon mom and frisky cubs
Were mucking up our pond before my eyes,
A hungry bunch of damned Beelzebubs
Devouring all our fish and leafy plants.
So much for all our neighborly romance.

A DANCING CHIHUAHUA NAMED ADELITA

Where else would a dancing chihuahua
Choose to dance, given half a chance,
But on Broadway in New York City?
Most likely it was Adelita's mistress,
Who adored her tiny pooch,
Who made the decision as to where
She might demonstrate Adelita's devotion
To Terpsichore, Goddess of the Dance.
After all, said mistress, costumer,
Adelita's choreographer and agent,
Is obviously the proper choice
As to where the dancing chihuahua
Might best perform her pirouettes
And other geometric niceties.

My wife and I strolled from our building
On the Upper West Side
To see a diverse circle,
Which the city seems often to produce
On its sidewalks everywhere.

We elbowed in and looked down,
And there she was, little Adelita,
Decked out in frilly pink tutu,
Beaded necklace, of course, to match
While *Jalousie* played
On a mini tape recorder.
With hardly a glitch
And ecstasy on her face,
Adelita weaved about
On her two hind legs
In perfect time to the beat.
Whoever said a chihuahua
Couldn't ace a tango?
Maybe next a flamenco
If castenets aren't required.

The performance ended,
But no hat was passed,
This being art for the sake of art,
Although there was applause aplenty.
Adelita dropped to all four paws,
Proud satisfaction on her face
As she awaited the treat
She knew would soon be hers.
Everyone of course was smiling,
Strangers all, as they paused a little longer,
Reluctant to go their way
And end this happy moment.

TRIBUTE TO A BUZZARD

Ugly beast with feathers and a face
That might make Mom consider birth control.
I had happened close upon him
While he, in the middle of the road,
Was dining on a squirrel
Whose road-crossing luck had just run out.
A bottle of Bordeaux and a napkin
Were the scene's sole missing props.

I drove off, chuckling between shudders,
Feeling handsome, superior and important,
King of the mightiest of beasts,
While gazing in a mirror at my perfection.
But then, as tends to happen at such moments,
I met my comeuppance perhaps a hundred feet
Above the trees just above the horizon.

There he was, that selfsame bird,
Or at least his sibling or cousin,
Describing perfect circles well this side of heaven.

No big effort, no heavy wing pumping,
Just wing-warping on the bank as
He in agile silence floated about,
A well defined dark figure,
A stubby, peculiar, floating T
Above the trees, below the sky,
Ever circling, silently with elegance
And magic on the invisible air.
A slow ballet against a cloud-flecked sky.

I stopped at the side of the road,
Deciding to watch his geometry,
Even while recalling his compatriot
A few miles back, the one
With the naked, wrinkled visage.
I knew what he was doing, foraging,
Sniffing out and viewing death
So that he might live.

In doing so, even as he spiraled down
To another scrumptious snack,
He gave the lie to the wisdom that proclaims
Only undertakers and coroners truly benefit
From the process and inevitability we call death.
This repulsive creature, graceful beyond reckoning,
Requiring death to enable life,
In living out his nature
Renders the world a healthier and a cleaner place.

DOG WITH ATTITUDE

I have a tiny dog whose attitude
Quite often spurs me on to unkind views
I pray won't lead to acts so very crude
I'd have no satisfactory excuse.
The problem is that he, by name Alphonse,
Or Alphie as he's known throughout our block,
Does lousy things while faking innocence.
"How cute," say all, but that's sheer poppycock.

They think my Yorkie's brave beyond belief
When he attacks the wolfhound down the street,
A brainless way to bring on utter grief
By trying to be wolfhound's luncheon meat.
Then when he jumps upon my couch to pee,
He turns and smiles to show his love for me.

MY PSYCHIATRIST

My best friends are mostly animals.
I do not mean the two-legged kind,
Although I have nothing against birds,
Either the ones who claim our trees
Or those that adorn my dinner plate.
I'm talking here about the four-legged kind,
Mammals, the fuzzy, friendly, faithful ones,
Although some cats of my acquaintance
Don't always qualify for the *friendly*
And the *faithful* aspects,
Unable or unwilling to get it through
Their egocentric skulls that a hand that feeds you
Ought just maybe occasionally to be licked,
Not ignored or raked to shreds.

Anyhow, down the street lives Harry,
Surely financial enemy of psychiatrists.
I mean, who needs to rent that couch
For a hundred bucks or more
When there's Harry, more than satisfied

With a nickel's worth of dog biscuit,
Or even less, a scratch behind an ear?
Harry, you see, is my neighbor's mutt,
A mix of, well, let's be fancy and say instead
A mélange of Lab and Shepherd and so on,
A virtual tail-thumping cornucopia
Of canines evolved to love and nurture humans;
In brief, a mélange both soulful and beautiful.

Harry is the neighborhood's resident psychiatrist.
Now we, my wife and I, are cat people, so-called,
Even though we don't on stormy nights morph
Into evil denizens of everyone's nightmares
And go prowling in search of victims
Chosen for their sweetness and innocence.
(Who would need to harm the other kind?)
But no, we are not such, we simply have cats
Because they do not need walking on winter morns
And, despite their frequent wishes to not be nice,
They do their hygienic manifestations into litter trays,
No doubt the right thing for the wrong reason;
Namely, to remain secretive and undetected.
And that is why we seek out Friend Harry,
When egos damaged by this or that,
When self-pity has us bobbing on a sea of doubt
Or foolish argument is pursued by guilt,
Or when we've looked into a mirror
And screamed silently in self-recognition,
Then that's when we visit Harry.

We stagger out our door, turn left
Toward Lafayette Street and the corner
Where Harry dwells with his family,
Smug folks well aware of the treasure they possess
And the envy they arouse up and down our block.
Yes, smug, and I don't blame them one bit,
For I'd be smug too were Harry mine.
But then again Harry is mine, and, a problem,
Everyone else's, too, when it would be nice
To think he is the way he is simply because of me,
Not just because he's democratically inclined.
Well, never mind, the main thing is that
Harry does exist, and so on this particular day
After everything's gone wrong for me
I hasten out the door, turn left and head for Harry.
He is there, glad to say, napping on his porch,
But seeing me he comes dashing out
Wriggling like a colony of hairy worms,
As eager for the scratch behind his ears
As I am eager to provide.

We talk a little about this and that,
With me of course leading surreptitiously
To what's really on my mind; namely, me.
I explain to him, haltingly at first,
That my wife and I have had a spat,
One as nasty and as silly as
Only the long-time married can achieve,
Knowing very well as they do
The way to each other's vulnerabilities.
Harry listens well, and when I stop my spiel
He removes his eyes from me and gazes

Most wisely, profoundly down.
Silence, a palpable silence, with Harry's gazing
Into the center of the earth.
"Well, Harry," say I at last, "what should I do?"
He looks up, obvious disappointment in his eyes,
Disappointment with me, of course.
A long moment passes hoisted again on silence,
And finally I say, "Okay, so I'm wrong,
Is that right, Harry? Tell me."
He looks at me, sadness tearing in his eyes,
And I know then what I must do.

"All right, Harry, thanks. As usual you're right."
He nuzzles his nose against me, telling me, "Yes."
It won't be easy returning home, opening the door
And pausing there a while to confess that,
Yes, she was right all along, and I was an ass.
Forgive? Forget? Carry on?
Of course, exactly what I know is right.
After all, didn't Harry's silence say it's so?

VIEWPOINTS

NIGHTMARE

We are, God says, supreme on planet earth.
It's we who dominate the other beasts
And scorn the futile thought of any dearth
Of His bequest, which yields our daily feasts.
We're bound to our unique supremacy.
Whatever else is there for us to do
But yield with thanks to God's philanthropy
And help ourselves to everything in view?

We do not smugly claim that less is more,
Insulting Him before His watchful eyes.
Instead we hear Him well, our humble chore:
We take, we use, we can't do otherwise.
Why is it then that every night I hear
Tyrannosaurs laugh loudly in my ear?

ALCHEMY REDUX

Statistics helps our economy grow,
Showing and knowing
Where a need lies lurking,
Because there is a way
To turn a need into gold.

Think not then that alchemy
Has long since had its day.
It is indeed alive and well,
With successes far beyond
What skeptics had to say.

Take for example terrorism,
A positive stroke of luck
If ever there was one,
Because new weapons
And military strategies
Cost beyond all reckoning.

Riches for some beyond calculation
Must follow on the heels of
Each terrorist gift.
In fact, it's the perfect product
Our alchemists discovered,
Ever renewing itself
By creating more terrorism
So that more weapons and such
Must then of course follow.

Same with prisons,
Universities of a sort,
Where crime can be improved
So that more prisons must be built
With attendant riches galore
Forecast by visionary alchemists,
Seeing poverty a glorious plus
Before turning its civic muck into gold,
So that crime of the street
Must, like poverty itself,
Be allowed to prosper and to grow
Into bigger and better prisons
Profitable for some well beyond
What our visionary alchemists

Dared to dream.

We have failed to give them their due,
Our alchemists, reciting the old lies
That denigrated these worthy souls
And declared them useless quacks.
Useless, indeed, when without them
Where would we be?
Let me tell you where:
Terrorism without profit,
Poverty and crime without profit,
And a world sworn to diminish both.
That's where we would be.
What a thought, a world not worth dwelling in,
And so gratitude to our alchemists,
Our visionaries who know dross when they see it
And roll it into gold.

WAR ON TERROR

Growth industries are hard to find,
And so those who lead us into such
Deserve our every accolade.
After all, they are the doers,
Not the whiny little takers,
Unpatriotic bloodsuckers draining our land
Of possibility itself,
The unwashed aided by educated
Smart-asses moaning about the poor,
About our rotting infrastructure,
About climate doing us in,
Our medical situation,
Our unhealthy air,
About our unhealthy water,
Fracking and oil pipelines,
About our student loans,
Our poverty
And other gross inequalities,

About Wall Street
And banks too big to fail;
In brief, about everything,
Pretending they speak for God
When those who really speak for Him
Are those whom God Himself
Has obviously appointed to recognize
His gifts to them,
Available for the taking.

Terrorism, for example,
One of the latest opportunities granted us.
By whom I am not certain,
But certainly by someone
Very much in tune with
Possibilities that could mean
Not thousands, mind you,
Not millions, mind you,
But billions, and, who knows,
Perhaps trillions of dollars in profits
Totally out of line.

To what do I refer?
What else, but drones and bases,
Spy planes and heavy bombers,
Armies, missiles, rifles, tanks, bombs,
Uniforms and spies beyond counting,
Generals and headquarters,
Contractors, torture cells, cooperating countries,
Secret missions, eavesdropping,
Soldiers stationed everywhere,
Special satellites, our own purchased politicians,
Co-opting foreign leaders here and there,
Who come expensive, don't you know?
The list goes on beyond imagining,
Dollars uncountable
Flowing into the coffers of the doers,
Those worthy ones aforementioned,
Investments difficult to record,
But paying off so that anyone
Who thinks that terrorism
Is a most unfortunate state of being
Should think again and realize
That here we have a patriotic avatar
Of such free-market meganomics
And wars against the unrighteous
That even the keenest neocon will be satisfied.

ARMS AND THE MAN

We are at war again - we never aren't.
Perhaps it is a civilized disease,
But jungle dwellers, too, seem to have learnt
That lopping off a head or two can please.
"Vile brutes," cry we, so very much advanced,
Whose drones and planes from sky-high purity
Discharge their instruments, with thought perchance
That those chopped up are guilty as can be.

Vast wealth for those who make our things of war,
But spears and arrow tips cost so much less,
So who can claim that jungle slayers are
Like us in finding war their prime largesse
When gain on severed heads is minuscule
Compared to that of planes and grimmer tools?

DIRTY WORD

The most obscene of obscene plagues is greed,
Which drives each host to sociopathic need
To place our minds like frogs in boiling pot,
Thus slowly melting them until there's not
A person left to call a human being;
Instead, the living dead, consumer, thing,
A gizmo shuffling here and there each day,
Assured that he and she still have a say.

The two are right and yet the two are wrong,
For both indeed do have a say so long
As what they say does not repudiate
The rules the greedy use to consecrate
Their methods which unfailingly augment
The swollen coffers of the one percent.

ONCE UPON A TIME

It's once upon a time for dreams that were
And are no more than smoke from yesterday.
It's all become, that dream, less than a blur,
A sparkling vision hurled so far away
Our City on the Hill cannot be seen
And, strange to tell, few seem to know it's so:
A haze of lies has fouled the once pristine
And overshadowed its resplendent glow.

Our dream was never halfway realized
Although there were those dazzling moments when
We sang, we marched, we dreamed, we fantasized
And swore we'd always try and try again.
But hope itself cannot help us succeed
If it lies crushed by lies and gold and greed.

STOLEN IDENTITY

We all it seems to me have enemies,
But there are those who do not ever think
That what reduces others to their knees
Could hurtle them as well toward the brink.
For instance, take my dear friend Anderson,
Beyond belief his care for everyone,
Protecting all from thug and charlatan,
And yet he, too, fell prey to dextrous cons.

Pretending to be friends of his, they scammed
My friend by stealing his identity.
He changed and swore to me that he'd be damned
If ever more he loved unthinkingly
And felt that people were innately good:
A loss, I think, for simple brotherhood.

EMILY KNEW

"I'm nobody. Who are you?" said Emily D.
"Are you nobody, too?"
And oh, did she ever know whereof she spoke.

Each and every night, aglow with importance,
Those pompous entitites, our Talking Heads,
Flood our TV screens, our sole escape,
Other than switching off the damn machine,
Being the commercials, and after those
You welcome back the bloviators.

Of course those reductio ad absurdums
Selling everything from erectile solutions
To happiness if you but choose the right paper towel,
Earn the money that our important ones need,
And then some, not unlike the monetary processes
Of our malevolent charlatans in Congress
Pleasing the plutocrats who own the country,
Doing the brisk manual labor required
To shovel clean their pathways to plusher riches.

Not that all are malevolent and disingenuous,
For some, both bloviators and elected ones,
Are honorable but stupid enough
To make those who grant them their sinecures
Cling to them in comfortable symbiosis.

Perhaps it's always been like this,
That anonymity is a univeral quicksand
Swallowing up by myriads the most of us,
And then, nature abhorring vacuums,
The extraordinary ones, swamp frogs all,
Emerge upon the surface to croak out
Their significance and sincerity.
Maybe Emily considered the plight
Of those so desperate to avoid
The abomination of anonymity
That they squirmed and clawed their way
To visibility, not pausing there,
But croaking out their wisdom
To all the knuckle-dragging fools
Wanting to know what they should believe
When these important ones declare,
"Look at us, hear us, we signify
And are here to serve you and you and you."

Let us, then, we the insignificant
In order to form a more perfect plausibility
Listen for the quieter ones, the humble ones
Who have not been purchased and won't be,
Who do not lie about even the obvious,
Who neither fear nor scorn, deceive nor mock
The most of us, the anonymous, who
Live and die and cry and laugh and need
Just like the quieter and the humbler ones,
Who know full well and act upon these truths
So that we need no longer heed the dreary
Croaking of those others.

THREE TAKES ON TOMORROW

1. The Cynic
Your talk of *future* I deem worthless.
My friends think so too.
Nothing more than unused time
Manipulated by opportunistic frauds.
How can anyone be so daft as
To hang it all on a loaded die or two?
Hope, then, you declare?
That delusion fashioned to buoy the drowning?
Hope rests on the far side of Mars, my friend,
Its product quite tangible...rhetorically,
Not unlike cotton candy,
Sickly cloying and even more ephemeral.
I admit, since you insist,
That we do have our problems,
But so what? For me
I tinker here and tinker there,
To ward off moral bores.
Besides, I am neither greedy nor puerile,
Always wishing foolishly for something better,
Like an avaricious ape groping for shiny baubles.

2. The Ever-Hopeful
Things can't be worse here, can they now?
Or perhaps they can be,
Which is why each morning I awake
Dreary, tired, longing for tomorrow.
A spin of the wheel, yes, and
Fortune may or may not be there,
But always worth a try even though
Spoil-sports swear the wheel is rigged
To favor the house.
I may be but a transient Irishman,
But still, rainbows do exist, don't they now?
And have leprechauns ever truly been disproved?
I've always fancied rainbows even over sunny morns,
When, as stated, I am dreary and desperate
And would gladly find the rainbow's end
On the other side of the horizon,
Which, alas, keeps a tad beyond my reach.
Yet I ask for nothing more because
Just to glimpse that pot of gold would mean
I was right after all.

3. The Pragmatist
The quest accounts as much as its conclusion,
My excuse to soldier on, my secret remedy
I frankly wish that many more shared with me.
Let me add, too, that a certain memory sustains me.
A creek, you see, near where we lived
Stank of chemicals from the upstream tannery,
Stank of bloated fish, of feces and refuse drifting,
An ugly, putrefying liquid corpse until one night
The tannery burned to the ground.
Then some irrascible, noisy old ladies, nuisances all,
Shamed any who would deny this opportunity:
No more tanneries, no more chemicals,
No more dead fish and garbage in our stream.
A bit of time, and one day we awoke puzzled.
Our accustomed stench had disappeared.
Instead, our stream giggled, sparkled, tickled the grasses
Clearly visible in its crystalline clarity,
Cool and clean to the touch,
Sweet-smelling, our new-born brook,
Alive with minnows and other sinuous things.

AFTERWORD

How does a poem originate? Does it spring from its writer's head like Athena from the head of her father Zeus, fully realized and ready to do battle? It could, I suppose, and sometimes does, but I suspect most writers work away until their words at least approach what they want to say, in the process creating sound, meaning and, yes, being. In my sonnet "Ghosts" I aim to reveal that our senses are a way to our past, to memories, to the ghosts, benevolent and otherwise, that waft through our consciousness; an image, for instance, a scent, a sound, whatever triggers a memory of a moment or of a person now gone. I know there have been times when, highly inspired, I wrote rapidly and brilliantly, full of joy, and completed the masterwork in short order. Reading it the following day, I felt embarrassed and either buried it in a sympathetic waste basket or vowed to hammer away and make it a viable poem rather than a poem that "writes itself."

It's long been cliché, the mantra that proclaims all writing to be autobiographical, but even the obvious might well bear repeating. That poem which captures something from the past, the writer's or someone else's that has attracted him or her, by filtering through the writer's mind or feeling, has become a part of that writer's being and is therefore autobiographical. A writer's take on his subject, love and hate, science and politics, life and death, war and peace, joy and sorrow, saints and sinners, however the writer imagines it, that writer is offering much of self, even though perhaps literal autobiographical aspects have been well disguised. Probably no writer can completely avoid revealing something of self as to sensibilities, outlooks, and even outright biographical facts, as in my poem "Grandma's Canary."

To make a sad joke, "Rhyme doesn't pay," and it really doesn't usually, but rhyme itself, a method, not the poem, can be a quintessential part of poetic expression. It helps create a poem's music while also framing and intensifying its meaning. Then, perhaps above all, there is the beat of a line, highly regular, say, as with iambic pentameter, or much less so with free verse, but nevertheless an inescapable pattern that carries you along. It seems to me that ultimately it is the cadence, the pulse, regular or otherwise, a poem's special heartbeat, that makes it a poem and not prose, even though, rarely, some prose is more or less scannable. The poems in this book exemplify different technical approaches. Some are Elizabethan, or Shakespearean, sonnets (fourteen lines of iambic pentameter - five beats of la-DA, la-DA per line) and a particular rhyme scheme, as in the poem "Visit to an Empty Space." Others use various kinds of rhyming patterns in free-verse lines that follow no one pattern but still create a sense of controlled sound; "Tropical Fish, A Brief Saga" illustrates this. Then there are poems herein that are completely unrhymed and that may or may not follow a precise beat, as with "I Am Ninety-Two." Why opt for one type and not another is difficult to say other than to suggest that the chosen approach seemed right when the piece was being written.

The forty-seven poems in this volume have emerged mostly from my own personal experiences and some from those of others I've known, as with "Out of Body." Forty-two of the poems were composed from the get-go over four months from mid-October of 2014; four existed as rough drafts from a while back, but were completed during the same time period; and one poem, "Kostas," was published long ago in my book of engaged political poetry, *Let Us Be Greek: Poems and Notes on a People's Struggle.* The thirty-seven poems of that book grew from our experiences in Greece where my wife and I were living and working when a coup d'état led by fascistic military men overthrew a democratically elected government. I've included it because even though it emerged from a specific moment of history, I believe it expresses in its particularities the universality of exile, in this case from a country the exile hungers for, but it could also be a person exiled from his family or even from himself. Universality in poetry, assuming the poem is accessible to its reader, I think is a mission of poetry almost beyond description, without which nothing else matters.

An interesting irony in the creation of universality is that a writer, by being specific and true to a moment or place or thing, is persuading the reader to realize through recognition and transference his or her own particular and special reality. It doesn't matter if that reader be far removed from the time, place and other details of the poem's references, he or she is the beneficiary of a wonderful literary paradox, that through the specific the universal may emerge. Take my comedic poem "A Midnight Nocturne," unfortunately quite autobiographical: Even a reader who might not know a raccoon from an aardvark should recognize that someone who was aspiring to impress his neighbors met his comeuppance and so failed to make the desired impression. Déjà vu? I hope so. Or then there are those who fancy cats and might be readily able to associate the antics of the feline in "Our Cat" with their own experiences. This poem grew from a moment when C.C., our cat of twelve years and old enough to know better, leaped upon a spot of sunlight to catch or kill it, and so the poem "A Dancing Chihuahua Named Adelita" emerged from our seeing many times a tiny NYC neighborhood pooch dressed in tutu and willing and able to dance on her hind legs. And of course there are moments removed from a physical happening, but instead instances of thoughts and feelings worth writing about and sharing through poetry's music and meaning. Such it is with "Goodbye, A Critique" and "Reaching." Each poem bears with it an image of my choice simply because I enjoy "seeing" a poem, my own included, and feeling it through several senses. My purpose is not to impose in any way the thrust of the image, my choice, on the reader, but simply to share a personal physical possibility and a way of feeling the poem. Perhaps not unlike a boy splashing barefoot through a warm puddle on a summer's day, I enjoy wallowing in a poem's images, its music, and all the things it is capable of. Besides, pictures are fun.

Our lives are kaleidoscopic, shards of moments that together form a mosaic. We can take a single minuscule shard from our life, or someone else's, or an entire mosaic, and breathe life into it so that it has substance and meaning, dimension and music. A number of the poems herein evolved from the voyages my life has been, both literal and figurative, and most likely all lives are. Thus do I recall a few of the countless shards of my life: my boyhood in Virginia – stumbling though school, doing nutty things, learning to fly and becoming a little less foolish; military service; college in Virginia and New York; travels to France and Greece and later residencies there; marriage lasting into six decades; living and teaching in Virginia, New Jersey, New York; children and grand-children; creating an antiques business specializing in the American Arts and Crafts Period (Stickley, etc.), and writing about it; volunteer worker in the Bronx Zoo; writing plays; our most recent move (some twenty in all) to Chapel Hill in North Carolina. So much to dream and think and write about: poems like "Mycenae At Dawn" emerging from travels; reactions to various conditions demanding response, leading to poems like "Arms and the Man" and "Three Takes on Tomorrow;" questions simple, yet hard to answer, confronting all of us, and so "Retirement Home" or "What You Don't Know" or "Love...?". In brief, every poem herein has evolved from a reality, even that of a dream, visible and tangible or hidden and unseen, but imprinted on heart or mind.

Most of these poems deal with the everyday, the ordinary, but as Walt Whitman once declared, a blade of grass is also a miracle. It is my deepest wish, then, that these poems attract, entertain, teach, amuse, speak directly to the emotions, even cause wonder, but above all that they be accessible and comprehensible to their readers and listeners and perhaps make the ordinary a little less so. It's why I wrote "Sonnet for the Rest of Us," a suggestion that poems should scare away no one, but rather, in profound service to the language of which they consist, greet one and all warmly and, in a sense, say, "Here we are for you."

Norman Weinstein
Chapel Hill, 2015

ACKNOWLEDGEMENTS

The Halcyon Marble background of the cover is used by permission of Sri Aurobindo Handmade Paper.

In addition to her cover painting, "Empty Chairs," the paintings accompanying the following poems are also by Emily Eve Weinstein and are included by her permission:

"Before the Storm"
"Efbee the Mysterious"
"Ghosts"
"Hanging Up the Clothes"
"Love?..."
"My Psychiatrist"
"Our Cat"
"Proof of Gravity"
"Raphael's Corner"

The painting "Kites" accompanying the poem "Reaching" is by Nathan Shapiro and is owned by the poet.

A number of photographs and drawings illustrating the following poems are used by permission of Can Stock Photo, Inc.:

"Backyard Nocturne"
"A Dancing Chihuahua named Adelita"
"Alchemy Redux"
"Cemetery In Normandy"
"Dirty Word"
"Dog With Attitude"
"Emily Knew"
"Farewell to New York"

"First Love"
"First Solo"
"Goodbye, A Critique"
"Grandchild"
"Grandma's Canary"
"Nightmare"
"Once Upon a Time"
"Out of Body"
"Sonnet for the Rest of Us"
"Stolen Identity"
"The Great Depression"
"The Rich Aren't Really So"
"Three Takes on Tomorrow"
"Tribute to a Buzzard"
"Tropical Fish"
"Visit to an Empty Space"
"Visit to Delos"
"War on Terror"
"What You Don't Know"

My very special thanks to John Patrick Grace, Executive Director of Publishers Place, Inc., who has greatly encouraged me in my writing and has unstintingly offered me his sound editing advice, his technical assistance, and of course his skill in bringing together the many elements that made this book possible.

ABOUT THE POET

Born and raised in Roanoke, Virginia, Norman Weinstein learned to fly at sixteen. He joined the U.S. Maritime Service and later the Army Air Force, where he became a newspaper correspondent with the Air Transport Command. Educated at Roanoke College (BA) and Columbia University (MA), he taught school for a number of years in his native state and in New York State. Then he moved with his family to Greece and later France, in both of which countries he continued to teach. In reaction to his experiences in Greece after a military junta overthrew the democratically elected government, he wrote a book of politically engaged poems, which was published under the title *Let Us Be Greek, Poems and Notes on a People's Struggle*.

In addition to his first love, poetry, much of his writing has been for the stage, and he has completed six full-length plays and more than twenty one-act plays, mostly comedies. Several of his plays have been Equity-showcased in New York, and a number have had staged readings there. In fact, a recent drama of his, *Gene Bullard, C'est Moi!*, about the world's first black combat aviator, had one of its many staged readings aboard the World War II aircraft carrier *Intrepid*, anchored in New York's Hudson River. His most recent play, *Ad Astra*, is a drama set in World War I, and he is currently working on two full-length comedies, *Once Upon a Future*, about aging and materially successful former hippies, and *Occupy Inner Ear*, a strange attempt to change mankind's direction for the better. He has eleven ebooks available, (including this book), consisting mostly of individual plays and collections of one-acters, along with two prose tales, both of which reference his granddaughters. All are briefly summarized on his web page at mytitles.net.

Over the years he has been a volunteer worker at the Bronx Zoo, involved in a special outreach program that took two reptiles, two birds and two mammals to nursing homes and hospices. Also he and his wife established an antiques business, during which time he was a feature writer for two nationally circulated decorative arts magazines. He and his wife recently moved to Chapel Hill, North Carolina, from New York City. He has three children and two grandchildren.